Conten

Contents 1

Introduction 5

Chapter 1: Understanding Digital Strategy in Education 9

    What is a Digital Strategy? 9

    Benefits of Digital Integration 10

    Challenges and Misconceptions 12

Chapter 2: Assigning the Right People 16

    Identifying Key Roles 19

    Selecting the Right Individuals 22

    Building a Team 24

Team Assignment Checklist 27

Chapter 3: Assessing the Current Landscape 30

    Needs Assessment 31

    Why Conduct a Needs Assessment? 31

    Steps in Conducting a Needs Assessment 34

    Stakeholder Engagement 39

    Setting Clear Goals 40

Current Landscape Assessment Checklist 43

Chapter 4: Developing a Vision and Strategic Framework 47

    Creating a Compelling Vision 48

    Example Vision Statement 49

    Developing a Strategic Framework 49

Communicating the Vision and Framework 50

Vision and Strategic Framework Checklist 53

Chapter 5: Implementing the Digital Strategy 57

Rolling Out Technology Initiatives 58

Supporting Professional Development 59

Monitoring Progress and Evaluating Success 61

Implementing the Digital Strategy Checklist 64

Chapter 6: Evaluating and Sustaining the Digital Strategy 69

The Importance of Evaluation 70

Ensuring Sustainability of the Digital Strategy 72

Celebrating Success and Sharing Outcomes 73

Evaluating and Sustaining the Digital Strategy Checklist 75

Chapter 7: The Future of Digital Strategy in Education 79

Emerging Technologies Shaping Education 80

Emphasising Equity and Access 81

The Role of Lifelong Learning 82

Future Readiness Checklist 84

Chapter 8: Sustaining and Evolving the Digital Strategy 88

The Importance of Continuous Improvement 88

Fostering a Culture of Innovation 90

Ensuring Long-Term Sustainability 91

Professional Development as a Constant 92

Expanding the Vision Over Time 93

Sustaining and Evolving the Digital Strategy Checklist 95

Appendices **100**

  Appendix A: Digital Strategy Glossary 100

  Appendix B: Sample Digital Strategy Templates.............................. 102

  Appendix C: Example Case Studies 106

  Appendix D: Frequently Asked Questions (FAQ) 116

Real-World Tech Tools Guide: A Practical Resource for Schools **118**

Introduction

Education is currently undergoing one of the most significant transformations in its history. Driven by rapid advancements in technology and evolving societal demands, the conventional classroom, once focused on teacher-led instruction, textbooks and passive learning, is being replaced by a more dynamic and interactive model, where technology plays a central role. The traditional model of education is being fundamentally reshaped.

This shift represents **education's biggest change** and **one of education's greatest challenges:** the move from static, one-size-fits-all learning to a model that promises a more personalised, digitally enhanced learning experience. Students are no longer confined to the limits of a physical classroom; they have access to a wealth of digital resources, collaborative platforms and real-time information at their fingertips at any time of the day. Teachers are now required to not just be providers of knowledge, but facilitators helping students navigate an increasingly digital world.

Schools must find ways to effectively integrate technology while ensuring equal access for all students, maintaining high educational standards and preparing learners for an uncertain future shaped by rapid technological change. Issues such as infrastructure, digital literacy, cybersecurity and the digital divide present hurdles that must be addressed to successfully implement a digital strategy. The true challenge lies not just in adopting new technologies but in using them to enhance learning outcomes, support educators and equip students with the skills they need to thrive in a future where adaptability and digital competence are essential. As education stands at a critical juncture, the choices made today will determine whether schools can successfully navigate this digital transformation or risk being left behind.

Choosing the wrong person to lead the implementation of a digital strategy can be incredibly costly, both in terms of time and money. I've seen it happen countless times; individuals who may not have the right vision, expertise, or ability to navigate the complexities of digital transformation end up making decisions that derail progress. The result is often wasted resources, delayed timelines and missed opportunities for meaningful change. A lack of strategic direction or technical knowledge can lead to purchasing the wrong technologies, misallocating budgets, or failing to provide the necessary training and support to staff. This not only causes frustration but also puts the entire project at risk of failing to meet its goals. It's crucial that the right individual, someone with both leadership skills and a deep understanding of technology in education, is put in charge to avoid these costly missteps.

This book is designed as a practical guide to help your educational institution successfully plan and implement a comprehensive digital strategy. While the process may initially seem daunting, for the right individual, this challenge presents an exciting opportunity to drive meaningful change and innovation in education. Embracing this transformation allows you to play a pivotal role in shaping a future-ready learning environment that benefits students, teachers and the broader school community.

Each section of this guide is crafted to provide clear, actionable steps, complete with checklists to ensure you're on track throughout the journey. Whether you are enhancing infrastructure, fostering digital literacy, or integrating new learning technologies, this book is here to support you, step by step, making the complex task of digital transformation both manageable and rewarding.

Chapter 1: Understanding Digital Strategy in Education

What is a Digital Strategy?

A digital strategy in education is a comprehensive plan that leverages technology to enhance teaching and learning processes, or to simplify even further, it's like having a roadmap for how schools can use technology to make learning better and more fun. It encompasses the integration of digital tools, resources and methodologies to create a more engaging, effective and personal educational experience for students.

"A digital strategy in education is a comprehensive plan that leverages technology to enhance teaching and learning processes"

This strategy is not just about introducing new devices or software; it involves a holistic approach that aligns technology with educational goals, curriculum standards and the needs of students, the teachers, the operational staff and any other members of the school community.

Benefits of Digital Integration

A well-designed digital strategy may enhance the learning experience by allowing educators to create interactive, engaging lessons using multimedia resources like videos, simulations and gamified learning, which cater to different learning styles and make education more inclusive. Technology also enables personalised learning, allowing students to learn at their own pace through dynamic platforms that adjust content difficulty based on individual performance, ensuring that every student gets the support they need. Incorporating digital tools boosts student engagement with gamification and allows a sense of community with online forums, collaborative projects and virtual classrooms.

Digital resources improve accessibility for all students, including those with disabilities, through tools like screen readers, speech-to-text software and captioned videos. Digital tools also make assessment and feedback more efficient, providing educators with the ability to give immediate feedback via online quizzes and interactive platforms, helping students identify areas for growth. A solid digital strategy equips students with the technological skills and critical thinking they need to thrive in an increasingly digital world whilst also considering all relevant stake holders of the school community.

Challenges and Misconceptions

Despite the many benefits, implementing a digital strategy in schools can present a range of challenges that need careful consideration and thoughtful planning. While many of the advantages of integrating technology into education are clear, there are several obstacles that schools may face during the process. These challenges often stem from a lack of resources, insufficient training, or resistance to change among staff and students. To overcome these barriers whilst still maintaining the support of the school community, it is crucial to have a clear understanding of common misconceptions about digital strategies and technology integration. Misunderstandings around the cost, complexity, or necessity of certain tools can create roadblocks, as can unrealistic expectations about immediate results. Addressing these misconceptions head-on allows schools to develop more effective solutions and ensure that the digital strategy is implemented successfully.

Technology Alone Will Solve Problems

One major misconception is that simply introducing technology will automatically improve education. In reality, effective integration requires thoughtful planning, training and support for both educators and students.

One-Size-Fits-All Solutions

Schools may believe that a single technology solution will work for everyone. However, each school and student body is unique. A successful digital strategy must consider the specific needs and contexts of the school community.

Resistance to Change

Change can be daunting for educators accustomed to traditional teaching methods. It is crucial to foster a culture that embraces innovation and supports teachers as they adapt to new technologies.

Budget Constraints

Schools may worry that implementing a digital strategy is too costly. While some technology investments require funding, there are many free or low-cost resources available that can significantly enhance educational experiences.

Security and Privacy Concerns

With increased digital engagement comes the responsibility to protect student data. It is essential to implement appropriate security measures and educate staff and students about online safety.

A digital strategy in education is essential for preparing students and schools for success in a rapidly changing world. Understanding the definition, benefits and challenges of digital integration is the first step in developing a successful approach. As educators, administrators and policymakers work together to embrace digital strategies, they can create enriched learning environments that empower students to thrive.

In the next chapter, we will explore the importance of assigning the right individuals to lead the implementation of digital strategies and how their roles can significantly impact the success of the initiative.

Chapter 2: Assigning the Right People

Implementing a digital strategy in schools is a multilayered and complex process that demands careful planning, thoughtful execution and a long-term commitment to adaptation and improvement. Success in this hinges on one of the most critical factors: ensuring the right people are in the right roles.

Without a strong, well-organised team, even the most well-conceived digital strategy is unlikely to reach its full potential. This chapter delves into the importance of identifying and assigning key individuals to lead the digital transformation and highlights that the strength of the team drives the overall success of the initiative.

We will explore how essential it is to define specific roles within the strategy, offering guidance on what each role entails and how to select the most suitable candidates. Building this strong team is not simply about filling positions on an organisational chart; it's about cultivating a group of individuals who are aligned in their vision, passionate about innovation and committed to the successful implementation of the digital strategy. Effective teamwork requires more than just technical skills, it also depends on collaboration, communication and a shared commitment to the school's educational goals.

While each role has its own distinct responsibilities, it is important to recognise that in many cases, one person may be able to take on multiple roles, especially in schools with limited resources. It is important to make sure that the workload is balanced and that no individual is overwhelmed. Understanding the differences between the roles is vital to creating a cohesive, efficient team. By clearly distinguishing the functions of each role while also allowing flexibility, schools can create a dynamic team capable of adapting to the evolving needs of the digital strategy. Ultimately, this chapter will offer a comprehensive guide to building and empowering a team that is well-equipped to lead a school's digital transformation.

Identifying Key Roles

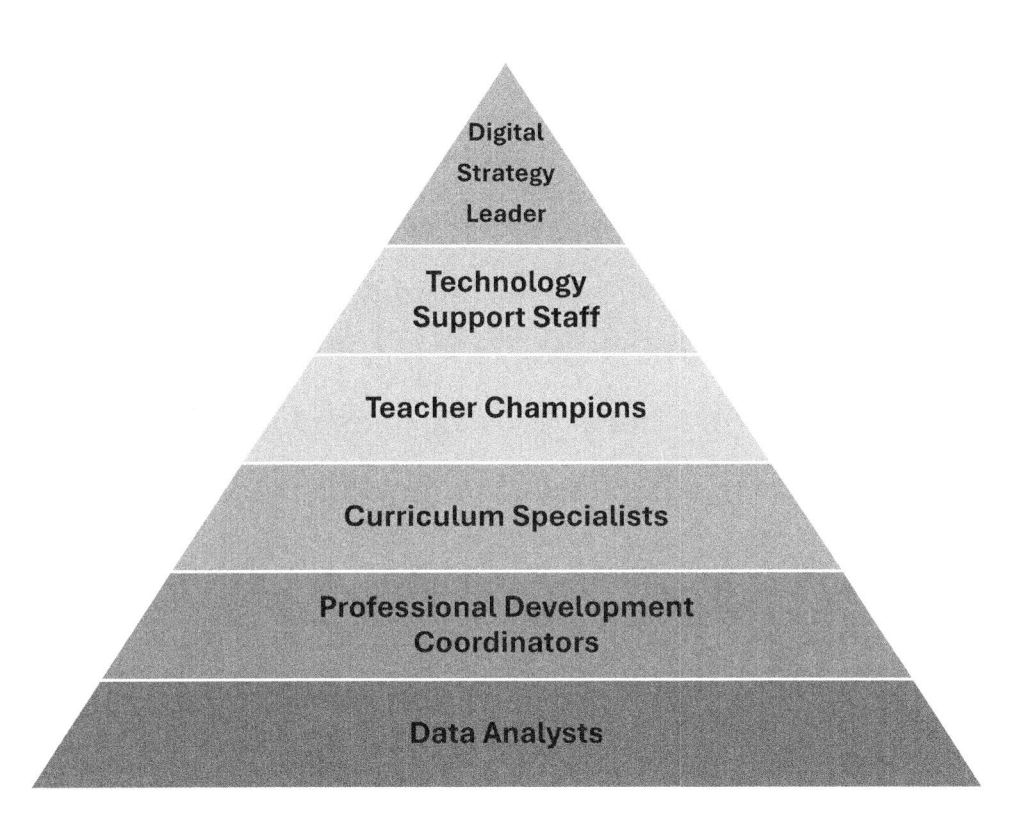

- Digital Strategy Leader
- Technology Support Staff
- Teacher Champions
- Curriculum Specialists
- Professional Development Coordinators
- Data Analysts

Digital Strategy Leader

This individual will serve as the driving force behind the digital strategy. The digital strategy leader should have a deep understanding of educational technology, experience in implementing digital initiatives and strong leadership skills. This role is crucial for aligning the digital strategy with the school's vision and ensuring that all stakeholders are on board.

Technology Support Staff

This team will provide technical support and maintenance for the digital tools and resources used in the school. Their expertise will ensure that teachers and students have reliable access to technology and can troubleshoot any issues that arise. These should be members of your academic staff rather than operational staff and will be fully supportive of the digital strategy.

Teacher Champions

These are educators who are passionate about technology and willing to explore new teaching methods. Teacher champions play a vital role in modelling effective use of technology in the classroom, mentoring their peers and providing feedback to the digital strategy leader on what works and what doesn't.

Curriculum Specialists

Curriculum specialists will help integrate digital tools into the existing schemes of work. They should be able to collaborate with teachers to develop lessons that leverage technology effectively while meeting educational standards.

Professional Development Coordinators

This role involves designing and facilitating training programs for staff. Professional development coordinators ensure that teachers receive ongoing support and training to build their digital literacy and confidence.

Data Analysts

In a data-driven approach, analysts play a crucial role in evaluating the effectiveness of the digital strategy. They collect, analyse and interpret data related to student performance, technology usage and overall program effectiveness, providing valuable insights for continuous improvement.

Selecting the Right Individuals

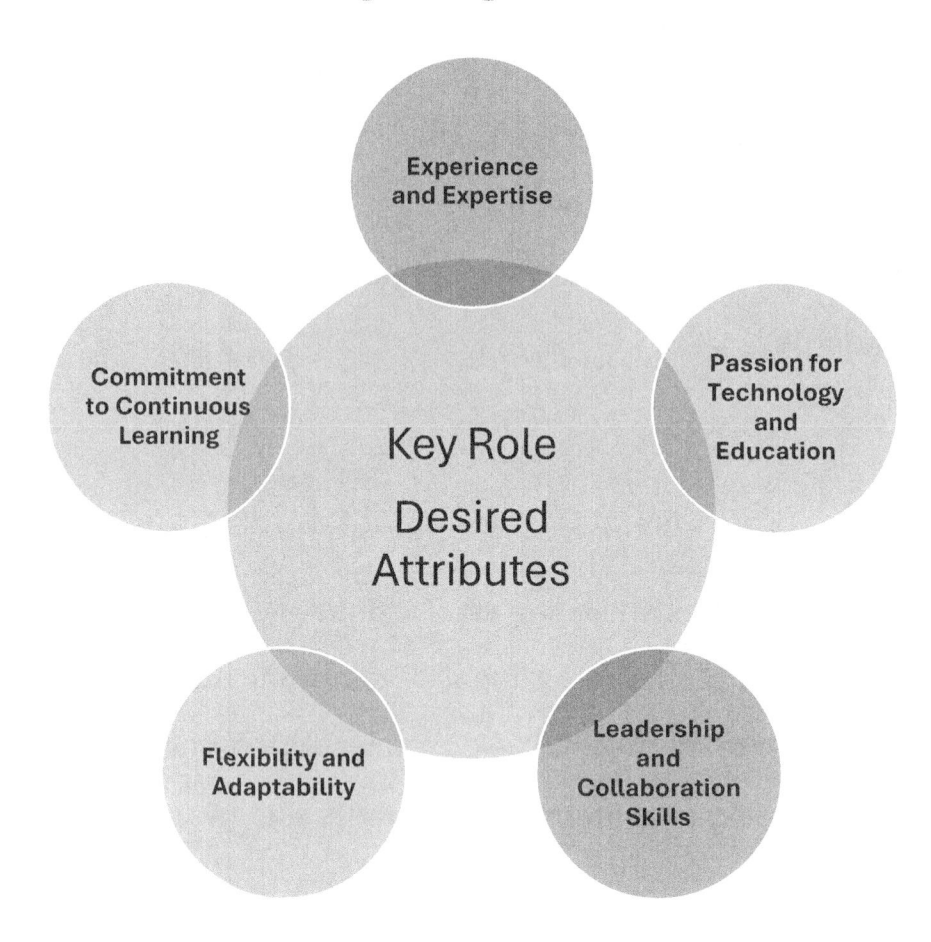

Key Role Desired Attributes:
- Experience and Expertise
- Passion for Technology and Education
- Leadership and Collaboration Skills
- Flexibility and Adaptability
- Commitment to Continuous Learning

Choosing the right individuals for these roles is crucial for the success of the digital strategy. The following criteria should be considered when selecting candidates:

Experience and Expertise

Look for individuals with relevant experience in education, technology integration, or specific areas related to the digital strategy. Their backgrounds will provide valuable insights and skills to the team.

Passion for Technology and Education

Candidates who are genuinely passionate about both technology and education will be more motivated to drive change and inspire others. Look for individuals who actively seek out new learning opportunities and stay updated on educational trends.

Leadership and Collaboration Skills

The ability to lead and collaborate is essential in a team environment. Candidates should demonstrate strong interpersonal skills, including the ability to communicate effectively, listen actively and build relationships with colleagues.

Flexibility and Adaptability

Digital strategies often require adjustments and changes along the way. Look for individuals who are open to feedback, willing to adapt to new ideas and comfortable navigating uncertainty.

Commitment to Continuous Learning

Technology and education are constantly evolving fields. Select candidates who are committed to their professional development and willing to engage in ongoing learning to improve their skills.

Building a Team

Once the key roles are identified and individuals selected, the next step is to build an aligned team that works effectively together. To foster collaboration and teamwork, it's important to establish clear goals, ensuring that everyone has a shared understanding of the digital strategy's objectives and purpose. Encouraging open communication is key; creating an environment where team members feel comfortable sharing ideas, asking questions and providing feedback through regular meetings makes this happen. Promoting collaboration by encouraging team members to work together, share resources and learn from each other's experiences can lead to innovative solutions and a stronger sense of community. Celebrating successes, both big and small, helps to boost morale and motivates the team to continue their efforts. Providing professional development opportunities through training and development programs can strengthen the team's skills and knowledge, enhancing their ability to effectively implement the digital strategy.

Assigning the right people to lead and implement a digital strategy is vital for success. By identifying key roles, selecting individuals based on specific criteria and fostering collaboration within the team, schools can create a strong foundation for digital transformation. As the journey continues, having committed and skilled individuals in place will help ensure that the digital strategy aligns with the school's vision and meets the needs of all stakeholders.

In the next chapter, we will explore how to assess the current landscape of technology and resources within the school, setting the stage for developing a robust digital strategy.

Digital Strategy Implementation: Team Assignment Checklist

Instructions:

Use this checklist to evaluate your school's readiness to assign the right individuals for your digital strategy implementation. Mark each item as **Yes** (Y), **No** (N), or **In Progress** (IP).

Criteria	Description	Y/N/IP
1. Identify Key Roles		
Digital Strategy Leader	Is there a dedicated leader for the digital strategy?	
Technology Support Staff	Have you identified staff responsible for tech support?	
Teacher Champions	Are there teachers who are passionate about using technology?	
Curriculum Specialists	Is there someone to align technology with the curriculum?	

Professional Development Coordinators	Do you have individuals focused on staff training?	
Data Analysts	Is there someone who can analyse data to assess effectiveness?	

2. Select the Right Individuals

Experience	Do candidates have relevant experience in education or tech?	
Passion	Are the candidates enthusiastic about technology and education?	
Leadership Skills	Do candidates demonstrate strong leadership and collaboration skills?	
Adaptability	Are the candidates flexible and open to feedback?	
Commitment	Do they show a willingness to engage in continuous learning?	

3. Build a Collaborative Team

Clear Goals	Are the goals of the digital strategy clearly defined?	
Open Communication	Is there a culture of open communication among team members?	
Promotion of Collaboration	Are team members encouraged to collaborate on projects?	
Celebration of Success	Do you have a plan to Recognise team achievements?	
Professional Development	Are there opportunities for ongoing training and development?	

Additional Notes:

Write down any specific actions or next steps based on your evaluations:	

Chapter 3: Assessing the Current Landscape

Before embarking on the journey of implementing a digital strategy in schools, it is essential to understand the existing landscape of technology, resources and educational practices. Conducting a thorough needs assessment will provide insights into the strengths and weaknesses of the current setup, help identify areas for improvement and ensure that the digital strategy aligns with the school's goals. This chapter will guide you through the process of assessing your school's current technological environment, engaging stakeholders and setting clear objectives for your digital strategy.

Needs Assessment

A needs assessment is a systematic process used to identify and understand the gap between the current conditions and the desired goals of an organisation. In the context of developing a digital strategy for a school, this process helps to ensure that the technology plan is tailored to meet the specific needs of the school community, including students, staff, operational staff and parents. A thorough needs assessment helps schools make informed decisions about resource allocation, infrastructure investments and professional development. It sets the stage for a digital strategy that enhances teaching, learning and operational efficiency.

Why Conduct a Needs Assessment?

Conducting a needs assessment is a critical first step in developing a school's digital strategy for several reasons. First, it ensures that digital tools and technologies are aligned with the school's educational goals, such as improving learning outcomes, personalising instruction and preparing students for their digital future. It also helps allocate resources by allowing schools to rank spending on tools, systems and training that will have the greatest impact, especially within limited budgets.

Involving students, staff, operational personnel and parents in the process of developing and implementing a digital strategy is crucial for fostering stakeholder buy-in. By engaging members from each element of the entire school community in meaningful ways, schools can ensure that the digital strategy is not only accepted but also actively supported by all involved. When students feel that their needs and learning preferences are considered, teachers have input into the tools and methods they will use in the classroom and parents understand how digital transformation will benefit their children, a collective sense of ownership emerges. This involvement leads to greater enthusiasm, cooperation and commitment to the success of the digital strategy. Stakeholder buy-in creates a shared sense of responsibility, encouraging all members of the school community to play their part in making the strategy work.

The assessment helps to identify gaps in the school's current digital capabilities. Schools may discover that they are working with outdated hardware, unreliable internet infrastructure, or that their teaching staff lacks sufficient training to fully utilise digital tools. These deficits can greatly hinder the effectiveness of any digital strategy, but by identifying them early, schools are able to prioritise and address these challenges head-on. This step is vital for making targeted improvements that ensure the technology is accessible, functional and capable of enhancing the learning experience for all students.

The assessment also helps schools address critical compliance and safety concerns, which are increasingly important in today's digital landscape. With technology playing a greater role in education, schools must be vigilant about protecting students' personal information and maintaining secure online environments. By uncovering potential vulnerabilities related to digital security, privacy and data management, schools can take proactive steps to mitigate risks. This includes ensuring compliance with GDPR and establishing protocols to safeguard students' information. Addressing these concerns not only builds trust among parents and staff but also makes the digital strategy more robust and sustainable in the long run.

Steps in Conducting a Needs Assessment

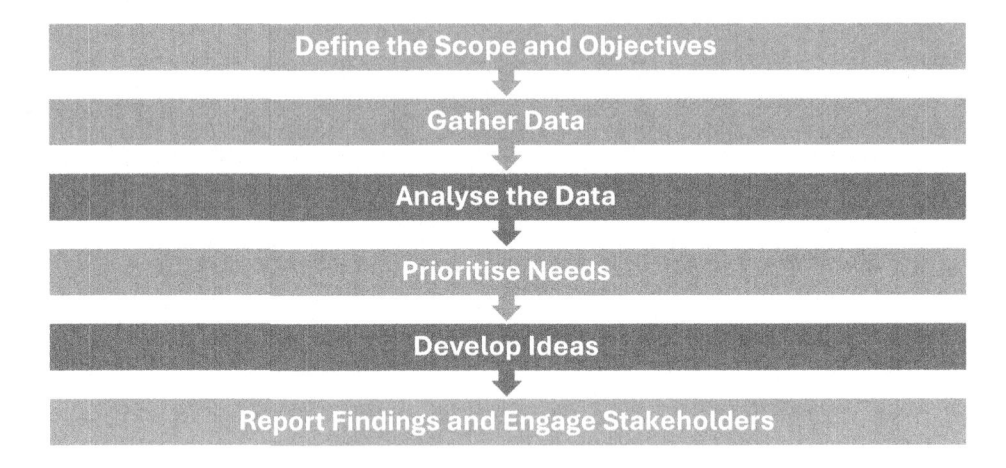

- Define the Scope and Objectives
- Gather Data
- Analyse the Data
- Prioritise Needs
- Develop Ideas
- Report Findings and Engage Stakeholders

Step 1

Define the Scope and Objectives

Begin by outlining the goals of the digital strategy and how the needs assessment will support these objectives. Consider key questions such as "what are the school's educational goals for integrating technology?" and "what specific learning outcomes does the school aim to achieve through digital tools?". Reflect on how technology could improve administrative processes, streamlining tasks to enhance overall efficiency. By addressing these questions, the digital strategy will align with the school's vision while targeting both instructional and operational improvements.

Step 2
Gather Data

Collect qualitative and quantitative data from a variety of sources to understand the current state of digital integration at the school. This can include distributing surveys to teachers, students and parents to collect feedback on the current use of technology in teaching, learning and operational efficiency. Conducting interviews or focus groups with key stakeholders such as administrators, IT staff, operational staff and department heads can provide deeper insights into the school's specific digital needs.

Classroom observations are also valuable for understanding how technology is currently being used and identifying any limitations in existing tools or teaching methods. Finally, conducting an audit of the school's existing technology infrastructure (covering hardware like computers and tablets, software, internet bandwidth, security protocols and IT support systems) will offer a comprehensive view of the school's digital readiness.

Step 3
Analyse the Data

Once the data is collected, it must be carefully analysed to identify the strengths, weaknesses, opportunities and threats (SWOT) related to the school's digital situation.

Key considerations during this analysis shows how current technology is being used, if the available tools are being used to their full potential and if there are areas where technology could be introduced to improve educational and operational outcomes. It's also important to assess the digital literacy and proficiency levels of teachers, students and operational staff to determine if additional training or professional development is required. Infrastructure gaps, such as inadequate hardware, slow internet connections, or a lack of IT support, should be identified to address technical shortcomings. A requirement at this stage is to consider the diverse learning needs of students, ensuring that the school's technology is accessible to all, including those with special educational needs, to provide an inclusive learning environment for every student.

Step 4

Prioritise Needs

Once the gaps have been identified, prioritise them based on their impact on the school's overall educational goals and their feasibility within the school's budget and resources. For example, upgrading the internet infrastructure might take precedence over purchasing new software if the current bandwidth is not sufficient to support existing tools. If teachers lack confidence in using technology, investing in professional development could be prioritised over acquiring new hardware.

Step 5

Develop Ideas

Based on the findings, develop recommendations that address the identified needs and are actionable.

Recommendations should be clear, achievable and aligned with the school's broader goals: "Invest in 1:1 devices for students to improve personalised learning", "Provide professional development sessions on using digital tools to differentiate instruction" or "Upgrade internet bandwidth to accommodate increased demand from online learning platforms."

Step 6
Report Findings and Engage Stakeholders

Present the results of the needs assessment to key decision-makers and stakeholders, including the school leadership team, teachers, students and parents. It's important to communicate the rationale behind the recommended actions and how they will contribute to achieving the school's goals.

A well-conducted needs assessment is the foundation of a successful digital strategy in schools. It ensures that the chosen digital solutions are relevant, sustainable and aligned with the school's educational vision. By engaging stakeholders, gathering comprehensive data and identifying key priorities, schools can create a digital environment that supports effective teaching and learning while optimising resources. Ultimately, a digital strategy grounded in a needs assessment is more likely to drive positive change, enhance student outcomes and ensure that the school is equipped to navigate the demands of a digital future.

Stakeholder Engagement

Engaging stakeholders is essential to ensure that the digital strategy aligns with the needs and priorities of the entire school community. Begin by identifying key stakeholders, such as teachers, staff, operational staff, students, parents, administrators and community members. Facilitate their participation through surveys, interviews, focus groups and workshops to gather feedback and insights. Encourage open dialogue by fostering an environment where stakeholders feel comfortable sharing their opinions and providing honest feedback. Communicate the findings of the needs assessment transparently, demonstrating that their input has been valued and considered in shaping the strategy.

Setting Clear Goals

Once the needs assessment is complete and stakeholders have been engaged, it is essential to set clear, measurable goals for your digital strategy. Well-defined goals provide direction and focus, making it easier to track progress and success.

Align with the School's Mission and Vision

Ensure that your digital strategy goals are aligned with the overall mission and vision of the school. This alignment helps create a cohesive approach to education.

Use the SMART Framework

Goals should be:

Specific	Clearly define what you want to achieve.
Measurable	Establish criteria for measuring progress and success.
Achievable	Set realistic goals that can be accomplished within a defined timeframe.
Relevant	Ensure that goals are meaningful and aligned with the needs of the school community.
Time-bound	Set deadlines for achieving each goal.

Involve Stakeholders

Include input from stakeholders when setting goals. This collaborative approach fosters buy-in and ensures that the goals reflect the needs of the entire school community.

Document and Share Goals

Write down the goals and share them with all stakeholders. This documentation serves as a reference point for tracking progress and holding individuals accountable.

Assessing the current landscape is a crucial step in implementing a successful digital strategy. By conducting a thorough needs assessment, engaging stakeholders and setting clear, measurable goals, schools can lay the groundwork for a digital transformation that meets the needs of students, teachers and the broader community.

Digital Strategy Implementation: Current Landscape Assessment Checklist

Instructions:

Use this checklist to evaluate your school's current technology landscape, engage stakeholders and set clear goals for your digital strategy implementation. Mark each item as **Yes** (Y), **No** (N), or **In Progress** (IP). Add comments as needed.

Assessment Components	Description	Y/N/IP	Comments
1. Conducting a Needs Assessment			
Defined Purpose	Have you clearly outlined the goals of the needs assessment?		
Data Collection Methods	Have you identified methods for data collection?		
Surveys Distributed	Have surveys or questionnaires		

	been distributed to stakeholders?		
Interviews Conducted	Have interviews or focus groups been conducted?		
Observations Made	Have classroom observations been completed?		
Data Analysis	Has the collected data been analysed for trends and patterns?		
Findings Summarised	Have you summarised the findings in a comprehensive report?		
2. Stakeholder Engagement			
Stakeholders Identified	Have you identified key stakeholders for engagement?		

Participation Facilitated	Have you created opportunities for stakeholders to participate?		
Open Dialogue Encouraged	Is there an environment fostering open communication?		
Findings Communicated	Have the findings been shared with all stakeholders?		
3. Setting Clear Goals			
Aligned with School Mission	Are your digital strategy goals aligned with the school's mission?		
SMART Framework Used	Have you used the SMART framework to define your goals?		
Stakeholder Involvement	Were stakeholders involved in the goal-setting process?		

Documented Goals	Are the goals documented and shared with stakeholders?		

Additional Notes:

Chapter 4: Developing a Vision and Strategic Framework

With a clear understanding of your school's current landscape and stakeholder needs, the next step in implementing a digital strategy is to develop a cohesive vision and strategic framework. A well-defined vision serves as a guiding star for the digital strategy, while a strategic framework outlines the steps and processes needed to achieve that vision. This chapter will explore how to create a compelling vision for digital integration in education, develop a strategic framework and ensure that both are communicated effectively to all stakeholders.

Creating a Compelling Vision

A vision is a forward-looking statement that outlines the school's desired future state in terms of digital integration. It provides inspiration, direction and clarity, guiding the alignment of efforts and resources.

To ensure the vision reflects the entire school community's values, engage teachers, administrators, students and parents in its creation. Focus on outcomes, considering what skills and competencies students should develop and how technology will enhance teaching and learning. The vision should be aspirational, motivating the school community to embrace change, yet concise and easily understood. Test and refine the vision by sharing it with stakeholders and incorporating their feedback.

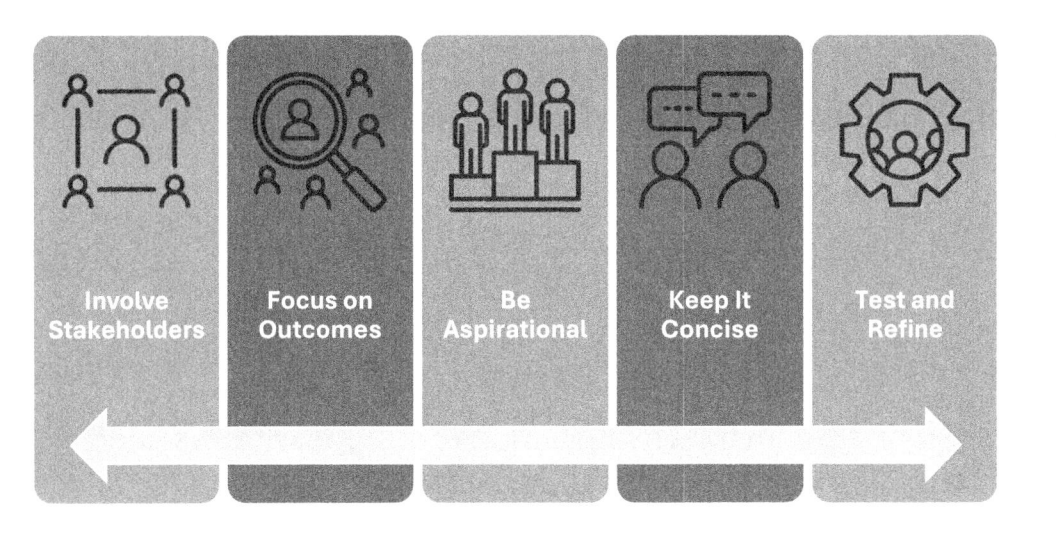

Involve Stakeholders	Focus on Outcomes	Be Aspirational	Keep It Concise	Test and Refine

Example Vision Statement

"Our school will empower every student to thrive in a digital world by fostering a culture of innovation, creativity and critical thinking through integrated technology in all learning experiences."

Developing a Strategic Framework

Once a vision is established, the next step is to create a strategic framework that outlines the goals, initiatives and action steps necessary to achieve that vision. This framework acts as a roadmap for implementation, providing structure to the digital strategy. First, set clear, measurable goals that align with the school's mission, focusing on areas like enhancing student engagement, improving digital literacy and upgrading infrastructure. Next, identify key initiatives such as implementing one-to-one devices or offering professional development for educators.

Break each initiative into actionable steps with assigned responsibilities and deadlines to ensure accountability. Create a timeline with short-term and long-term milestones to track progress and assess the necessary resources (technology, training, funding and personnel) to ensure the plan is well-supported and achievable.

Communicating the Vision and Framework

Effective communication is crucial to the successful implementation of a digital strategy. To ensure that all stakeholders are informed and engaged, use multiple communication channels, such as emails, newsletters, meetings and workshops to share the vision and strategic framework.

Since different stakeholders may prefer various formats, this approach ensures broad reach. Visual aids like infographics, posters or slide presentations can simplify complex ideas and make the strategy more engaging. Hosting discussions, forums or focus groups allows stakeholders to actively participate, fostering a sense of ownership and collaboration.

It's also essential to solicit feedback, inviting suggestions and demonstrating that everyone's input is valued. Finally, regularly revisiting the vision and framework in communications keeps it top-of-mind and reinforces collective commitment to successfully implementing the digital strategy.

Developing a compelling vision and strategic framework is a vital foundation for the successful implementation of a digital strategy in schools. A clear and inspiring vision serves as a guiding beacon, providing both direction and motivation for the entire school community. The strategic framework breaks down that vision into actionable steps, detailing the goals, initiatives and resources necessary to bring it to life.

Engaging stakeholders in this process (teachers, students, parents and operational staff) ensures the vision reflects the diverse needs and aspirations of the community, encouraging a shared sense of purpose and ownership. Effective communication throughout this phase is crucial, as it builds trust and commitment toward the digital transformation journey. In the following chapter, we will delve into how to implement the digital strategy with practical guidance, covering best practices for rolling out technology initiatives, supporting educators and students and ensuring the long-term success of the strategy.

Digital Strategy Implementation: Vision and Strategic Framework Checklist

Instructions:

Use this checklist to evaluate the effectiveness of your school's vision and strategic framework for digital strategy implementation. Mark each item as **Yes** (Y), **No** (N), or **In Progress** (IP).

Vision and Framework Components	Description	Y/N/IP	Comments
1. Creating a Compelling Vision			
Stakeholder Involvement	Were key stakeholders involved in the visioning process?		
Outcome Focused	Does the vision emphasise the desired outcomes of digital integration?		
Aspirational	Is the vision statement		

	ambitious yet achievable?		
Conciseness	Is the vision statement clear and concise?		
Tested and Refined	Has the vision been shared and refined based on stakeholder feedback?		

2. Developing a Strategic Framework

Clear Goals	Are the goals specific, measurable and aligned with the school's mission?		
Key Initiatives Identified	Have major initiatives needed to achieve the goals been identified?		
Action Steps Established	Are there actionable steps defined for each initiative?		

Timeline Created	Is there a timeline for implementing initiatives and action steps?		
Resources Allocated	Have the necessary resources for implementation been identified and secured?		
3. Communicating the Vision and Framework			
Multiple Communication Channels Used	Have you used various methods to communicate the vision and framework?		
Visual Aids Created	Have you developed visual representations of the vision and framework?		
Stakeholder Engagement in Dialogue	Have you engaged stakeholders in discussions about the vision and framework?		

Feedback Solicited	Have you invited feedback on the vision and framework from stakeholders?		
Commitment Reinforced	Is there a plan to regularly revisit and reinforce the vision and framework?		

Additional Notes:

Write down any specific actions or next steps based on your evaluations:	

Chapter 5: Implementing the Digital Strategy

With a compelling vision and a strategic framework in place, the next crucial step is to implement the digital strategy effectively. This phase involves translating goals into actionable steps, rolling out technology initiatives, providing ongoing support and evaluating progress. Successful implementation requires careful planning, collaboration among stakeholders and a commitment to continuous improvement.

Rolling Out Technology Initiatives

When implementing a digital strategy, it's essential to assess the potential impact of each initiative. Prioritise those that will significantly enhance teaching and learning, aligning closely with the school's goals and addressing identified needs. Once priorities are set, create a detailed timeline for the rollout, outlining key milestones and deadlines to ensure the implementation stays organised and on track. Consider launching pilot programs for new technologies or initiatives. Piloting provides an opportunity to test the effectiveness of each initiative, gather feedback and make necessary adjustments before moving to full-scale implementation.

To ensure the success of a digital strategy, first evaluate the school's current technological infrastructure, including hardware, software, internet connectivity and network security, to determine if it can support new initiatives. If gaps are identified, prioritise the necessary upgrades to ensure that all devices and platforms are reliable, accessible and meet the needs of both staff and students.

Establish a dedicated tech support team to assist with troubleshooting and ongoing maintenance throughout the rollout process. Make sure all stakeholders are aware of how to access technical support when needed to minimise disruptions.

Supporting Professional Development

Professional development is essential for equipping educators with the skills and knowledge to integrate technology into their teaching practices. To ensure its effectiveness, start by tailoring training programs to meet specific needs.

Use feedback from the needs assessment to identify areas where teachers need support, such as digital tools, instructional strategies or digital citizenship. Offer diverse formats for professional development, including workshops, online courses, peer coaching and collaborative planning sessions, to accommodate different learning styles and schedules. Additionally, promote a culture of continuous learning by encouraging ongoing professional development opportunities, where teachers can share experiences and best practices, fostering an environment of collaboration and growth.

To enhance professional development and foster collaboration, schools can establish Professional Learning Communities (PLCs) where teachers support each other in integrating technology. Mentorship programs can also be used to pair experienced educators with those less confident in digital tools.

Celebrating successes motivates others to follow suit. For student engagement, creating a student-centred environment is key. This is done by incorporating student voice in technology decisions, offering choice and agency in how students demonstrate learning and promoting collaboration through online tools and platforms. These strategies encourage creativity, ownership and teamwork, ensuring successful digital strategy implementation in the classroom.

Authentic learning fosters relevance and engagement. Design learning experiences that connect technology to real-world challenges and problems. Incorporate gamified elements into learning experiences to make them more engaging and teach students about responsible technology use, digital ethics and online safety.

Monitoring Progress and Evaluating Success

To ensure that the digital strategy is effective, schools must regularly monitor progress and evaluate outcomes. Identify specific key performance indicators (KPIs) related to the goals established in the strategic framework. These could include metrics such as student engagement levels, technology usage rates and academic performance. Gather data through surveys, assessments and usage reports to evaluate progress toward achieving KPIs, this regular data collection will help identify trends and areas for improvement. Continuously analyse the collected data to assess the effectiveness of the digital strategy and reflect on successes and challenges to inform your future planning.

Creating a culture of innovation requires intentional strategies and actions. Promote the idea that failure is a part of the learning process and celebrate efforts and encourage educators to learn from their mistakes; allow teachers to pilot new instructional strategies or technologies without fear of judgment. Embrace flexibility in the implementation process and if certain initiatives are not achieving the desired outcomes, be willing to adjust or modify them. Engage stakeholders in reflecting on the progress of the digital strategy by gathering feedback and suggestions for improvement from teachers, students and parents. Share the results of evaluations with all stakeholders as transparency fosters trust and encourages ongoing collaboration in improving digital strategy implementation.

Implementing a digital strategy in schools is a complex but rewarding process. By rolling out technology initiatives thoughtfully, supporting professional development, engaging students and continuously monitoring progress, schools can create a transformative learning environment that harnesses the power of technology.

Digital Strategy Implementation:

Implementing the Digital Strategy Checklist

Implementation Components	Description	Y/N/IP	Comments
1. Rolling Out Technology Initiatives			
Initiatives Prioritised	Have you prioritised initiatives based on impact?		
Implementation Timeline Created	Is there a timeline for the rollout of each initiative?		
Pilot Programs Implemented	Have pilot programs been conducted for new technologies?		
Infrastructure Needs Evaluated	Has the current technological infrastructure been assessed?		

Upgrades Made	Have necessary infrastructure upgrades been implemented?		
Technical Support Maintained	Is there dedicated technical support available for staff and students?		
2. Supporting Professional Development			
Training Needs Assessed	Have you assessed training needs among educators?		
Diverse Training Formats Offered	Are professional development opportunities available in various formats?		
Continuous Learning Culture Fostered	Is there a culture of continuous learning for educators?		
Collaborative Learning	Have Professional Learning		

Communities Established	Communities (PLCs) been formed?		
Successes Celebrated	Are successes in technology integration recognised and celebrated?		
3. Engaging Students			
Student Voice Incorporated	Are students involved in decisions regarding technology use?		
Choice and Agency Provided	Are students allowed to choose how they demonstrate their learning?		
Collaboration Encouraged	Is technology used to promote collaboration among students?		
Authentic Learning	Are real-world issues integrated		

Experiences Integrated	into learning experiences?		
Digital Citizenship Promoted	Are students taught about responsible technology use and digital citizenship?		
4. Monitoring Progress and Evaluating Success			
Key Performance Indicators (KPIs) Defined	Have you defined specific KPIs for measuring success?		
Data Collected Regularly	Is data being collected regularly to evaluate progress?		
Data Analysed and Reflected Upon	Is the collected data analysed to assess effectiveness?		
Stakeholders Involved in Reflection	Are stakeholders engaged in		

	reflecting on progress?		
Outcomes Communicated	Are results shared with all stakeholders for transparency?		

Additional Notes:

Chapter 6: Evaluating and Sustaining the Digital Strategy

Implementing a digital strategy in schools is a significant undertaking that requires ongoing evaluation and sustainability efforts. While initial implementation can be exciting and filled with momentum, maintaining the energy and effectiveness of the strategy over time is equally crucial. This chapter focuses on the importance of continuous evaluation, the strategies for assessing the effectiveness of the digital initiatives and how to ensure that the digital strategy remains sustainable and relevant in the ever-evolving educational landscape.

The Importance of Evaluation

Regular evaluation is essential for understanding the impact of the digital strategy on teaching and learning. It provides insights into what is working, what isn't and what adjustments may be necessary. Evaluation provides the data needed to make informed decisions regarding the effectiveness of digital initiatives and their alignment with educational goals. Regular evaluations hold all stakeholders accountable for their roles in implementing and supporting the digital strategy and fosters a culture of continuous improvement, allowing schools to refine their approaches based on evidence and feedback.

Evaluation processes can engage students, educators, parents and the community, fostering collaboration and shared ownership of the digital strategy. Sharing evaluation results with stakeholders builds trust and encourages a collective commitment to the strategy's success.

Effective evaluation requires a systematic approach that includes both qualitative and quantitative methods. Establish specific, measurable KPIs related to the goals of the digital strategy. Examples include student engagement levels, academic performance and technology usage rates. Utilise surveys and feedback mechanisms to gather input from educators, students and parents regarding their experiences with the digital initiatives.

Employ various data collection methods, including assessments, observations, interviews and focus groups. This diversity will provide a comprehensive view of the strategy's impact. Conduct regular analysis of collected data to identify trends, successes and areas needing improvement. Use data visualisation tools to present findings clearly.

Encourage educators and administrators to engage in reflective practices, examining the effectiveness of their methods and sharing insights with colleagues. Develop action plans based on evaluation findings. Identify specific

[71]

steps for improvement, assign responsibilities and establish timelines for implementation.

Ensuring Sustainability of the Digital Strategy

Sustaining a digital strategy requires ongoing commitment, resource allocation and strategic planning. School leaders must demonstrate a clear commitment to the digital strategy by actively supporting initiatives and advocating for resources. Encourage educators to take ownership of their roles in implementing the strategy. Provide opportunities for leadership and professional growth within the team.

Offer continuous professional development opportunities that align with the evolving needs of educators and the digital landscape. This includes workshops, conferences and online courses. Implement mentorship programs where experienced educators can support their colleagues in using technology effectively and innovatively.

Allocate a portion of the school budget for ongoing technology updates, maintenance and training. Ensure resources are available for future digital initiatives. Explore partnerships with local businesses, organisations and educational institutions to secure additional resources and support for digital initiatives.

Celebrating Success and Sharing Outcomes

Recognising and celebrating successes is crucial for sustaining enthusiasm and motivation within the school community. Create opportunities to showcase student projects, innovative teaching practices and successful technology integration through school events, newsletters and social media. Establish recognition programs for educators and students who demonstrate exceptional innovation and collaboration in their digital learning journeys.

Utilise collaborative platforms for educators to share best practices, success stories and lessons learned from implementing the digital strategy. Involve parents and community members in discussions about the successes and impacts of the digital strategy, fostering a sense of pride and support.

Evaluating and sustaining the digital strategy is an ongoing process that requires commitment, reflection and collaboration among all stakeholders. By establishing clear evaluation criteria, engaging in regular data analysis and ensuring strong leadership and resource allocation, schools can maintain the momentum of their digital initiatives. Celebrating successes and sharing outcomes fosters a positive culture that encourages innovation and collaboration. In the next chapter, we will explore the future of digital strategy in education, including emerging trends and technologies that can shape the learning landscape.

Digital Strategy Implementation: Evaluating and Sustaining the Digital Strategy Checklist

Use this checklist for evaluating and sustaining the digital strategy. Mark each item as **Yes** (Y), **No** (N), or **In Progress** (IP).

Evaluation and Sustainability Components	Description	Y/N/IP	Comments
1. Defining Evaluation Criteria			
Key Performance Indicators (KPIs) Established	Have you established clear KPIs related to the digital strategy goals?		
Surveys and Feedback Mechanisms Created	Are there regular surveys or feedback mechanisms in place to gather input?		
2. Collecting and Analysing Data			

Diverse Data Collection Methods Used	Are multiple methods (assessments, observations, interviews) used for data collection?		
Regular Data Analysis Conducted	Is data analysed regularly to identify trends and areas for improvement?		
3. Reflecting and Acting on Data			
Reflective Practices Encouraged	Are reflective practices encouraged among educators and staff?		
Action Plans Developed Based on Evaluation Findings	Are there action plans created from evaluation results?		
Ensuring Sustainability			

Leadership Commitment Evident	Is there visible commitment from school leadership to the digital strategy?		
Continuous Professional Development Offered	Are ongoing professional development opportunities available for staff?		
Resources Allocated for Technology Maintenance	Is there a budget for ongoing technology updates and maintenance?		
4. Celebrating Success and Sharing Outcomes			
Achievements Recognised	Are there opportunities to showcase and celebrate achievements in the digital strategy?		
Best Practices Shared	Are best practices shared among		

	educators and the community?		
Community Engagement Encouraged	Is there community involvement in celebrating and discussing the digital strategy's successes?		

Additional Notes:

Chapter 7: The Future of Digital Strategy in Education

As we look toward the future of education, digital strategies will continue to evolve, shaping and redefining how learning is experienced, delivered and accessed. New technologies such as artificial intelligence, virtual and augmented reality, and advanced data analytics are creating opportunities for increasingly personalised and immersive educational experiences. At the same time, shifts in educational paradigms call for a digital approach that is both flexible and inclusive, catering to a wide range of learning needs.

Emerging Technologies Shaping Education

The landscape of education is being reshaped by a variety of emerging technologies. Understanding these advancements will help educators and administrators make informed decisions about integrating them into their digital strategies.

AI has the potential to create personalised learning experiences for students by analysing their performance data and adapting instruction to meet individual needs. Machine learning algorithms can automate administrative tasks, such as grading and scheduling, allowing educators to focus more on teaching.

VR and AR can create immersive learning environments that engage students in ways traditional classrooms cannot, allowing for exploration of complex concepts in a hands-on manner. These technologies can simulate real-world scenarios, enabling students to practice skills in safe, controlled environments.

Emphasising Equity and Access

As digital strategies continue to evolve, it is crucial to prioritise equity and access to ensure that all students can benefit from technological advancements.

Schools must strive to provide all students with access to devices and reliable internet connectivity, particularly in underserved communities. Ensure that digital resources and technologies are designed with inclusivity in mind, catering to the diverse needs of all learners, including those with disabilities.

Incorporating culturally relevant content into digital resources helps students see themselves reflected in their learning materials, fostering engagement and belonging. Collaborating with community organisations and stakeholders can enhance the relevance of educational content and ensure that it resonates with students' experiences.

The Role of Lifelong Learning

In a rapidly changing world, the concept of lifelong learning is more important than ever. Preparing students for future challenges requires instilling a growth mindset and a commitment to continuous learning.

Digital strategies should emphasise the development of critical thinking and problem-solving skills, empowering students to navigate complex issues. Schools must teach students how to collaborate effectively in digital environments and communicate their ideas clearly. Digital strategies should promote self-directed learning, encouraging students to take ownership of their education and pursue their interests; providing access to online learning platforms allows students to explore subjects beyond the traditional curriculum, supporting their passions and interests.

The future of digital strategy in education is filled with possibilities and challenges. By embracing emerging technologies, prioritising equity and access and fostering a culture of lifelong learning, schools can create engaging and inclusive learning environments for all students. As we move forward, it is essential to remain adaptable and open to change, continuously reflecting on our practices and seeking innovative solutions.

Digital Strategy Implementation: Future Readiness Checklist

Instructions:

Use this checklist to evaluate your school's readiness for future digital strategies. Mark each item as **Yes** (Y), **No** (N), or **In Progress** (IP).

Future Readiness Components	Description	Y/N/IP	Comments
1. Emerging Technologies			
AI and Machine Learning Considered	Have you explored the potential of AI for personalised learning?		
VR and AR Utilised or considered	Are VR and AR technologies integrated on considered with the curriculum?		
Learning Analytics Implemented	Are learning analytics used to		

		drive instructional decisions?		
2. Equity and Access				
	Devices and Connectivity Provided	Is there equitable access to devices and internet connectivity for all students?		
	Inclusive Digital Resources Developed	Are digital resources designed to be inclusive for diverse learners?		
	Culturally Relevant Content Integrated	Is culturally relevant content incorporated into learning materials?		
3. Lifelong Learning Emphasised				
	Critical Skills Development Focused	Does the digital strategy prioritise critical thinking and problem-solving skills?		

Self-Directed Learning Encouraged	Are students encouraged to take ownership of their learning?		
4. Educator Preparation			
Professional Development Offered	Are ongoing professional development opportunities available for educators?		
Collaborative Learning Communities Established	Are networks for educators to share best practices in place?		
Growth Mindset Encouraged	Is a growth mindset modelled and encouraged among educators?		
Additional Notes:			

| Write down any specific actions or next steps based on your evaluations: | |

Chapter 8: Sustaining and Evolving the Digital Strategy

The successful implementation of a digital strategy is a major achievement for any school. However, it's essential to recognise that reaching this milestone is not the end, it's the beginning of an ongoing journey. In a rapidly evolving digital world, a digital strategy must be continuously nurtured, adapted and expanded to remain relevant and effective.

The Importance of Continuous Improvement

One of the most common pitfalls after implementing a digital strategy is the belief that the work is complete. However, education and technology are dynamic fields, constantly evolving with new tools, challenges and opportunities. The pace of technological change is rapid. Tools that are cutting-edge today may become outdated tomorrow. Schools must commit to regularly reviewing their technology stack and exploring new tools that enhance teaching and learning.

As new tools and platforms emerge, consider piloting them in small settings to assess their relevance and effectiveness before full implementation. As student populations and their needs change over time, so too must the digital strategies that support them. Regularly evaluate whether your digital tools, platforms and teaching methodologies are meeting the diverse needs of learners.

Educational paradigms evolve and schools need to stay aligned with modern pedagogical trends. Whether it's the rise of personalised learning, competency-based education, or inquiry-based learning, a digital strategy must adapt accordingly.

Fostering a Culture of Innovation

For a digital strategy to remain sustainable and effective, schools must cultivate a mindset of ongoing innovation and exploration. Encouraging educators and students to be curious, creative and willing to experiment with new approaches ensures that digital learning remains fresh and impactful. Give teachers the freedom to explore and experiment with new digital tools and teaching methods without fear of failure. Innovation often arises from trial and error. Recognise and celebrate educators who demonstrate creativity in using digital tools, fostering a positive environment where innovation is encouraged.

Students can be incredible sources of inspiration when it comes to using technology creatively. Invite them to share their ideas on how to improve digital learning environments. Encourage students to take ownership of their learning by leading digital projects or initiatives.

Ensuring Long-Term Sustainability

Sustaining a digital strategy requires careful planning, resource allocation and long-term commitment from leadership, educators and the wider school community. Set up a system for annual or biannual reviews of your digital strategy to assess its effectiveness, relevance and impact on student outcomes. Use data and feedback to guide these reviews. As part of the review process, adjust goals and objectives to reflect changes in technology, education policy, or school needs.

Sustainable digital strategies require ongoing funding for updates, maintenance and training. Ensure that your school's budget includes a line for technology maintenance and upgrades. Explore funding opportunities through grants, partnerships, or community sponsorships to support the long-term sustainability of the digital strategy.

Professional Development as a Constant

Ongoing professional development is key to keeping the digital strategy alive and evolving. As new technologies emerge and educational goals shift, educators must remain adaptable and continue to develop their skills. Offer regular professional development sessions to help educators stay up to date with the latest tools and instructional strategies. This training should be personalised to their needs and aligned with school goals. Create or maintain professional learning communities where educators can share insights, challenges and successes with digital strategies. Peer learning is a powerful way to keep momentum going.

School leaders also need ongoing training to understand new digital trends and how they can support their teams effectively. Digital leadership is crucial for long-term strategy success. Develop mentorship programs where more experienced educators can support those newer to digital tools and strategies.

Expanding the Vision Over Time

Once a solid foundation is in place, schools should explore ways to expand their digital strategy over time. This may involve deepening the integration of technology into the curriculum, exploring interdisciplinary projects, or even expanding the digital strategy to include community engagement or extracurricular activities. Explore ways to use digital tools to integrate learning across subjects, such as combining coding with art, or using data analysis in history lessons.

Consider expanding your digital strategy to include global collaboration projects, where students can work with peers from around the world, gaining cross-cultural skills and global awareness.

Engage parents and the broader community in your digital strategy. This could include offering workshops, creating student showcases of digital projects, or forming partnerships with local organisations.

The journey to implementing a digital strategy is an ongoing one. While reaching initial goals is an accomplishment, sustaining and evolving the strategy is key to ensuring its long-term success. By fostering a culture of continuous improvement, encouraging innovation and maintaining a commitment to professional development and reflection, schools can keep their digital strategies dynamic and responsive to the needs of both students and educators. Schools that embrace this journey, rather than treating it as a destination, will be better positioned to prepare their students for the challenges and opportunities ahead. So, keep moving forward, stay curious and remember: the work doesn't end here, it only continues to evolve.

Digital Strategy Implementation: Sustaining and Evolving the Digital Strategy Checklist

Instructions:

Use this checklist to evaluate your school's efforts to sustain, adapt and evolve its digital strategy. Mark each item as **Yes** (Y), **No** (N), or **In Progress** (IP).

Sustainability and Evolution Components	Description	Y/N/IP	Comments
1. Continuous Improvement			
Regular Technology Reviews	Do you regularly review and update the school's technology tools to ensure they are current and effective?		
Piloting New Tools	Are you testing and piloting new technologies		

	before full implementation?		
Adapting to Educational Changes	Does your digital strategy adapt to changes in educational needs, pedagogical trends, or student demographics?		

2. Fostering a Culture of Innovation

Encouraging Educator Innovation	Do educators feel empowered to experiment with new digital tools and teaching methods?		
Recognising Innovative Practices	Are you recognising and celebrating educators who show creativity in digital learning?		
Student Involvement in Innovation	Are students given opportunities to suggest or lead digital initiatives?		

| Student-Led Projects | Are student-led digital projects encouraged and supported? | | |

3. Long-Term Sustainability

Annual Strategy Review	Do you conduct annual reviews of your digital strategy to evaluate its success and areas for improvement?		
Adjusting Goals	Are goals and objectives adjusted based on feedback, data, or changes in the school environment?		
Ongoing Funding Secured	Is there a sustainable budget for maintaining and upgrading digital tools and resources?		

Grants or Partnerships for Support	Have you explored partnerships or grants to support the long-term sustainability of your digital strategy?		
4. Professional Development			
Continuous Training for Educators	Are regular training opportunities provided to keep educators updated on digital tools and teaching strategies?		
Professional Learning Communities (PLCs)	Are educators part of PLCs that foster collaboration and the sharing of best practices for digital strategies?		
Leadership Development	Are school leaders receiving training to better understand and support digital strategies?		

Mentorship Programs	Are mentorship programs in place to help educators newer to digital tools grow and develop?		
5. Expanding the Vision			
Interdisciplinary Curriculum Integration	Are digital tools used to promote interdisciplinary learning and collaboration across subjects?		
Global Learning Opportunities	Have you expanded digital projects to include global collaboration or interaction with peers worldwide?		
Additional Notes:			

Appendices

Appendix A: Digital Strategy Glossary

Understanding key terms is essential when navigating digital transformation. This glossary defines some of the most important terms used in the digital strategy space

1:1 Program: A program where each student is provided with a personal device, such as a laptop or tablet, to use for learning activities.

Blended Learning: A teaching model that combines online and face-to-face instruction, allowing students to engage with digital resources and in-person teaching.

BYOD (Bring Your Own Device): A policy that allows students to bring and use their own digital devices in the classroom.

Cloud Computing: Storing and accessing data and applications over the internet instead of on local devices or servers.

Digital Citizenship: The responsible use of technology by students, including understanding ethical use, privacy and online safety.

Digital Literacy: The ability to use digital tools effectively and critically, including finding, evaluating and creating information online.

Flipped Classroom: A teaching model where students engage with instructional content, such as videos or readings, at home, and then participate in activities or discussions in the classroom.

Learning Management System (LMS): A software platform that supports the management and delivery of educational content, resources and assessments.

Open Educational Resources (OER): Free, openly licensed educational materials that can be used for teaching, learning and research.

STEAM: An educational approach that incorporates Science, Technology, Engineering, the Arts and Mathematics into learning.

Appendix B: Sample Digital Strategy Templates

This section provides sample templates that can be adapted for a school's digital strategy planning and implementation. You can download any of these templates at www.digitalstrategy.school

1. Digital Strategy Planning Template

Component	Details	Responsible Person	Timeline	Notes
Vision Statement				
Current Technology Assessment				
Goals and Objectives				
Stakeholder Engagement Plan				
Technology Selection and Budget				

Professional Development Plan				
Implementation Timeline				
Monitoring and Evaluation Plan				

2. Professional Development Needs Assessment Template

Skill Area	Required Proficiency Level	Current Proficiency Level	Training Needed? (Y/N)	Notes
Digital Literacy				
LMS Use				
Digital Tools for Collaboration				
Assessment Tools				

| Classroom Management Tools | | | | |

3. Technology Review Template

Technology/Tool	Purpose	Current Use	Effectiveness (1-5)	Notes
Learning Management System (LMS)	Manage lessons and assignments	Widely used by all staff	4	
Classroom Devices	Student learning tools (e.g., Chromebooks)	Mixed usage	3	
Digital Assessment Tools	Assessments and quizzes online	Rarely used	2	

Appendix C: Example Case Studies

Case studies offer valuable insights into how other schools have implemented successful digital strategies. These examples highlight challenges, solutions and best practices.

School A: Building a 1:1 Device Program

Challenge: A school with limited funding wanted to move to a 1:1 device program to support blended learning.

Solution: By applying for grants, leveraging community support and gradually introducing the program, the school implemented a successful 1:1 device program over three years.

Outcome: Increased student engagement, improved digital literacy and equitable access to learning resources.

School B: Professional Development for Digital Tools

Challenge: Teachers were hesitant to adopt new technology due to a lack of confidence and training.

Solution: The school introduced a continuous professional development program focused on specific tools like Google Classroom and digital portfolios.

Outcome: Teachers became more confident in using technology, leading to more innovative lesson plans and improved student outcomes.

School C: Enhancing Parental Engagement Through Digital Tools

Challenge: Parents were not regularly engaging with the school, making communication about student progress and school events difficult. The school's traditional methods of communication like printed newsletters and occasional parent-teacher meetings, were insufficient and often missed.

Solution: The school introduced a digital parent portal and mobile app, which allowed parents to access real-time updates on their child's progress, attendance, homework and school events. Alongside this, they trained both teachers and parents on how to use these tools effectively.

Outcome: Parental engagement increased significantly. Parents were able to stay informed, ask questions and actively participate in their child's education. This led to better communication between the school and families, as well as improvements in student attendance and overall performance.

School D: Implementing a Flipped Classroom Model

Challenge: Teachers were struggling to cover the entire curriculum due to time constraints, leaving little room for personalised instruction or deeper student engagement during class time.

Solution: The school adopted a **flipped classroom model**, where students were provided with video lessons and readings to complete at home. In-class time was then used for collaborative projects, discussions and personalised support from the teacher. Teachers received training on how to create high-quality video lessons and structure in-class activities effectively.

Outcome: Students were more prepared and engaged in classroom discussions. The flipped model allowed for deeper exploration of topics and more one-on-one support for struggling students. Teachers reported a significant improvement in student understanding, particularly for complex subjects.

School E: Overcoming Infrastructure Limitations with Cloud Computing

Challenge: A rural school with limited budget and outdated hardware found it challenging to keep up with software updates, manage data storage and offer technology-enhanced learning experiences.

Solution: The school moved many of its resources to cloud-based services such as Google Workspace and Microsoft OneDrive. They also implemented virtual desktops that allowed students to access school software and files from home, reducing the need for constant hardware updates.

Outcome: By utilising cloud computing, the school improved efficiency and reduced hardware costs. Students and staff could access important resources from any location with internet access, leading to improved flexibility in learning and administration. The school's IT team also spent less time on maintenance and more time supporting digital initiatives.

School F: Introducing Gamified Learning to Increase Student Engagement

Challenge: The school noticed declining student engagement, particularly in core subjects like math and science. Traditional teaching methods weren't resonating with students and attendance for these subjects was lower than average.

Solution: The school introduced **gamified learning** using platforms like **Kahoot!** and **Blooket** to make learning more interactive and enjoyable. Teachers were trained in how to integrate game mechanics (such as point systems, levels and rewards) into their lessons to increase engagement and motivation.

Outcome: Student participation and enthusiasm increased noticeably, particularly in subjects that had previously been seen as challenging or "boring." Students began collaborating more during lessons and taking ownership of their learning progress. Attendance for these subjects improved and teachers noticed an increase in retention and comprehension.

School G: Using Data Analytics to Personalise Learning

Challenge: The school wanted to improve academic outcomes but lacked a way to track student performance in real time. Teachers were spending a lot of time manually grading and analysing student work, which delayed the ability to provide timely interventions.

Solution: The school implemented a **data analytics system** within its Learning Management System (LMS) to track student performance automatically. Teachers used the platform to access real-time data on student progress and identify those who needed additional support. Predictive analytics were also used to forecast which students were at risk of falling behind.

Outcome: Teachers were able to provide personalised interventions earlier, leading to noticeable improvements in student outcomes. The data-driven approach allowed the school to identify trends in performance, adjust teaching strategies and target areas for improvement. The system also reduced the administrative burden on teachers, allowing them to focus more on teaching.

School H: Building Digital Citizenship and Online Safety Programs

Challenge: With the increased use of technology, the school observed that students were engaging in unsafe online behaviour, such as cyberbullying and oversharing personal information. The school needed to address these issues and ensure students were practicing safe, responsible digital citizenship.

Solution: The school implemented a **digital citizenship curriculum**, educating students on online ethics, safety and privacy. They partnered with local organisations specialising in cyber safety and held workshops for both students and parents. Teachers were trained to integrate lessons on digital ethics into their subjects.

Outcome: The school saw a significant reduction in online incidents such as cyberbullying. Students became more aware of the potential dangers of their online actions and many adopted safer practices. Parents appreciated the school's proactive approach and students reported feeling more confident navigating the digital world.

School I: Hybrid Learning for Inclusive Education

Challenge: The school faced the challenge of accommodating students with different learning needs, including students who required extended absences due to health issues. They needed a solution that allowed these students to stay engaged without falling behind.

Solution: The school implemented a **hybrid learning model**, offering both in-person and online learning options. They used platforms like Zoom for live lessons and recorded content for students to access at their own pace.

Assistive technologies were also introduced to support students with disabilities.

Outcome: The hybrid learning model provided flexibility for students who needed it, ensuring that no one was left behind due to physical or learning challenges. Teachers could offer personalised support and students were able to maintain a consistent learning experience regardless of their situation. The approach fostered a more inclusive environment for all learners.

School J: Scaling Professional Development for Digital Skills

Challenge: Teachers in a large school academy trust had varying levels of digital proficiency. Some were highly skilled in using technology, while others struggled with even basic digital tools. The school needed a scalable, cost-effective way to provide differentiated professional development.

Solution: The school adopted an **online professional development platform** that allowed teachers to complete courses at their own pace. The platform included courses on various digital tools, classroom technology integration and advanced techniques like data-driven instruction. Mentorship programs were also introduced, pairing tech-savvy teachers with those who needed more support.

Outcome: Teachers improved their digital skills at their own pace and overall tech competency across the trust increased. The platform allowed teachers to choose courses based on their individual needs, leading to higher engagement and better application of technology in the classroom. The mentorship program fostered a culture of collaboration and professional growth.

Appendix D: Frequently Asked Questions (FAQ)

How do we ensure that all students have access to digital devices?

Schools can implement BYOD policies, apply for grants, seek community partnerships, or provide device loan programs to ensure all students have access to digital tools.

How do we keep up with fast-changing technology?

Regularly reviewing the school's digital tools and encouraging ongoing professional development for teachers helps keep pace with technological advances.

What if some teachers resist the use of technology?

Provide targeted professional development, mentorship and opportunities for teachers to see the benefits of technology through hands-on examples. It's also important to create a supportive environment where teachers feel comfortable experimenting with digital tools.

How can we measure the success of our digital strategy?

Establish clear goals and use data-driven approaches to measure outcomes such as student engagement, learning outcomes and teacher adoption of digital tools.

Real-World Tech Tools Guide: A Practical Resource for Schools

This guide will help schools identify and choose the best technology tools to support their digital strategy. Tools are organised by category, with a brief overview of their purpose, popular options and tips for effective implementation.

LMS Platforms:

A **Learning Management System (LMS)** is a platform that enables the management, delivery and tracking of online learning. It centralises content, assessments and communication, allowing teachers to manage lessons and interact with students.

Google Classroom: A free, user-friendly tool that integrates with other Google Workspace apps (Docs, Drive, etc.). **Strengths**: Easy to use, especially for schools already using Google services. **Limitations**: Less feature-rich compared to some paid platforms. **Tip**: Use Google Meet for live video classes and integrate Google Forms for quizzes.

Microsoft Teams for Education: Combines LMS features with robust collaboration tools, including video conferencing, file sharing and assignments. **Strengths**: Deep integration with Microsoft Office tools (Word, Excel, PowerPoint). **Limitations**: Can be complex for new users due to its many features. **Tip**: Leverage Microsoft OneNote Class Notebook for collaborative student workspaces.

Moodle: An open-source, customisable LMS used by many educational institutions worldwide. **Strengths**: Fully customisable and scalable for large schools. **Limitations**: Requires more technical expertise to set up and maintain. **Tip**: Use Moodle's extensive plugin library to tailor the platform to your school's needs.

Implementation Tips: Start with a pilot group of teachers and students to get feedback before rolling it out school wide and provide training sessions for teachers to maximise LMS features, like automated grading and analytics.

Communication and Collaboration Tools

These tools enable better communication and collaboration among students, teachers and administrators, both in and out of the classroom.

Slack: A messaging platform that allows for organised communication through channels, direct messages and file sharing. **Strengths**: Efficient team communication, quick updates and file sharing. **Limitations**: May be too complex for younger students or small schools. **Tip**: Create specific channels for subjects, grades, or projects to keep communication organised.

Zoom: A widely used video conferencing tool for virtual meetings and online classes. **Strengths**: Reliable, high-quality video conferencing with breakout room capabilities. **Limitations**: Can consume a lot of bandwidth and requires good internet connectivity. **Tip**: Use breakout rooms to facilitate group work and encourage student participation.

Microsoft Teams: Beyond its LMS capabilities, Microsoft Teams excels in group communication and collaboration. **Strengths**: Tight integration with Microsoft's productivity suite. **Limitations**: Requires a Microsoft ecosystem for full functionality. **Tip**: Use the chat and file collaboration tools for project-based learning.

Implementation Tips: Set clear guidelines for communication (e.g., expectations for response times, appropriate use of channels). Use collaboration tools to foster group work and peer learning in both synchronous and asynchronous settings.

Assessment Tools

These tools allow teachers to create and manage assessments, provide instant feedback and track student progress.

Google Forms: A simple and flexible tool for creating quizzes, surveys and feedback forms. **Strengths**: Automatically grades multiple-choice quizzes, integrates with Google Classroom. **Limitations**: Limited question types for complex assessments. **Tip**: Use the "response validation" feature to provide instant feedback on incorrect answers.

Kahoot!: A game-based learning platform where teachers can create interactive quizzes that engage students in a fun way. **Strengths**: Highly engaging, promotes competition and participation. **Limitations**: Best suited for formative assessments rather than in-depth testing. **Tip**: Use Kahoot! to review material before exams in a fun and interactive way.

Edpuzzle: Allows teachers to turn any video into an interactive lesson by embedding questions and tracking student responses. **Strengths**: Engages students with multimedia while providing insights into their understanding. **Limitations**: Limited features in the free version. **Tip**: Use Edpuzzle for flipped classroom models to reinforce learning outside class time.

Implementation Tips: Choose tools that offer automatic grading to save teachers time. Use a mix of assessment types (quizzes, polls and video responses) to cater to different learning styles.

Content Creation Tools

Teachers and students alike can use content creation tools to produce presentations, videos and multimedia content that enhance learning.

Canva: A graphic design tool that allows users to create presentations, posters, infographics and more. **Strengths**: Easy to use, even for those without design experience, with many templates. **Limitations**: Limited customisation options in the free version. **Tip**: Use Canva for student assignments like presentations or digital portfolios.

Adobe Spark: A suite of creative tools for creating videos, graphics and web pages. **Strengths**: Great for creating polished, professional-looking multimedia projects. **Limitations**: Some features require a paid subscription. **Tip**: Use Spark to create digital storytelling projects or explainer videos for class topics.

Powtoon: An easy-to-use platform for creating animated presentations and videos. **Strengths**: Engages students by allowing them to create their own animated content. **Limitations**: Longer videos require a paid plan. **Tip**: Encourage students to use Powtoon for projects where they explain a concept or event.

Implementation Tips: Use content creation tools to foster creativity and deeper learning, encouraging students to demonstrate their understanding through multimedia projects. Provide clear guidelines and rubrics for multimedia assignments to ensure that technology enhances learning rather than distracting from it.

Data and Analytics Tools

These tools help schools collect and analyse data to inform decisions, track student progress and improve teaching strategies.

Power BI: A data visualisation and analytics tool by Microsoft that helps schools track performance, attendance and engagement data. **Strengths**: Robust data analysis and reporting features. **Limitations**: Requires training for effective use. **Tip**: Use Power BI to create dashboards that visualise student performance trends over time.

Google Analytics Overview: A tool for tracking website traffic, student engagement on LMS platforms and more. **Strengths**: Offers detailed insights into how digital resources are used. **Limitations**: Requires setup and monitoring and the sheer amount of data can be overwhelming. **Tip**: Track which resources (videos, quizzes, lessons) students engage with most to identify what works best.

Printed in Great Britain
by Amazon